DATE DUE

MAY 1 6 1989	NOV 3 0 1988
MAY 2 2 1991	DEC 1 7 1988
DEC 6 1992	
JAN 1 1993	MAR 2 2 1999
DEC 1 3 1994	AUG 0 5 1999
JUL 2 2 1996	MAR - 4 2004
DEC 3 0 1996	AUG 1 6 2004
APR 0 7 1997	DEC 2 7 2004
	MAY 1 3 2005
OCT 3 1 1997	DEC 0 2 2005
DEC 1 5 1997	JUN 1 1 2009
JAN 0 6 1998	DEC 1 4 2009
FEB 2 4 1998	JAN 0 8 2010
APR 1 3	FEB 0 2 2010
APR 2 0 1998	
JUN 1 5 1998	
MAY 2010	

HIGHSMITH 45-220

Ring of Fire

And the Hawaiian Islands and Iceland

by Alice Gilbreath

Dillon Press, Inc.   Minneapolis, Minnesota 55415

To Tommie Sue and Pat

Library of Congress Cataloging in Publication Data

Gilbreath, Alice Thompson.
   Ring of Fire and the Hawaiian Islands and Iceland.
   Bibliography: p.
   Includes index.
   Summary: Explains how volcanoes erupt and the work
of scientists who study volcanoes, and describes some
well-known eruptions.
   1. Volcanoes—Pacific Ocean Region—Juvenile litera-
ture.   2. Volcanoes—Iceland—Juvenile literature.
[1. Volcanoes] I. Title.
QE524.G55   1985   551.2'1   85-6971
ISBN 0-87518-302-6

Dillon Press, Inc., 242 Portland Avenue South
Minneapolis, Minnesota 55415

Printed in the United States of America
1 2 3 4 5 6 7 8 9 10 93 92 91 90 89 88 87 86

Contents

Acknowledgments

The author wishes to thank Mark S. Manwaring, Surface Exploration Geologist, Phillips Petroleum Company, for checking this manuscript and for his helpful suggestions.

The photographs are reproduced through the courtesy of the Consulate General of Iceland; Pall Imsland; H. Olafsson; William P. Sterne, Jr.; S. Thorarinsson; the U.S. Geological Survey (R.H. Finch, J.D. Friedman, J.D. Griggs, J.G. Moore, D.W. Peterson, J. Rosenbaum, K. Segerstrom, H.T. Stearns, and R.E. Wilcox, photographers); and Don Yager.

 Volcano Facts

Location on Earth:
Three out of five volcanoes are found in the Pacific Ocean and on the land in and around it; the Ring of Fire has 500 or more active volcanoes

Largest Eruptions of This Century:
Katmai, Alaska—1912
Besimjannyi, Kamchatka (The Soviet Union)—1956

Greatest Known Natural Explosion:
Krakatoa (Indonesia)—1883

World's Tallest Mountain (Measured from Base to Peak):
Mauna Kea (extinct volcano on the island of Hawaii); it stands 30,000 feet (9,150 meters) from the ocean floor (16,000 feet are below the ocean's surface, and 14,000 feet are above the ocean's surface)

Lava Flows:
Since 1500, about one-third of all the world's new lava has erupted in Iceland

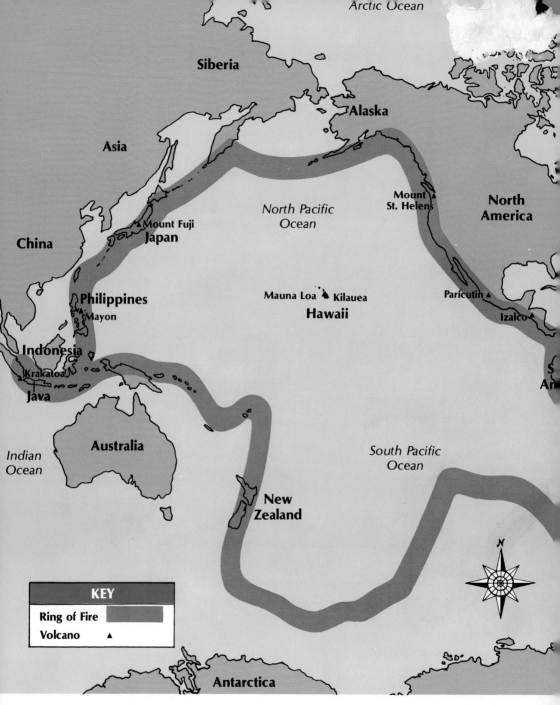

This map shows the path followed by the Ring of Fire around the edge of the Pacific Ocean and some of the major volcanoes that lie within it. The earthquake and volcanic activity in this narrow zone is more intense than anywhere else in the world.

# 1 The Big, Fiery Loop

While the Pacific Ocean may look calm and peaceful at the surface, explosive activity constantly takes place in its depths. **Earthquakes*** shake wide areas. **Volcanoes** erupt from the ocean floor. New islands appear as underwater mountains break the ocean's surface.

Suppose you could loop a huge rope along the edges of the continents and islands around the Pacific Ocean. The rope would be lying on top of most of the earthquake zones and most of the **active volcanoes** of the world. In fact, 500 or more active volcanoes lie in this explosive belt.

Such an enormous loop would be 30,000 miles (50,000 kilometers) long. If you tied a knot at each active volcano, the rope would have 500 knots. And if the knots were the same distance apart, there would be a knot every 60 miles (100 kilometers) of the loop.

Within a short time—perhaps, within hours—at least one of these volcanoes would erupt. Ocean and

*Words in **bold type** are explained in the glossary at the end of this book.

An eruption of Parícutin, a Mexican volcano in the Ring of Fire.

land lying under this fiery loop have the most intense earthquake and volcanic activity in the world. Earthquakes have shaken this region and volcanoes have erupted here so often that the edges of the continents and the islands surrounding the Pacific Ocean are known as the **Ring of Fire**.

A good place to locate a starting point on the Ring of Fire is at the southern tip of South America. It extends northward up the coasts of South America, Central America, and North America to Alaska. Then it circles westward through the Aleutian Islands to the Soviet Union's Pacific coast, and southward down the coast and islands of Asia, through Japan, the Philippines, Indonesia, New Guinea, and New Zealand.

Some volcanic **eruptions** in the Ring of Fire are much more powerful than others. These are very explosive and quickly destroy everything in their paths. Many people have been killed by volcanic eruptions or earthquakes. Others have been swept into the ocean by giant ocean waves that followed volcanic eruptions.

On the other hand, some eruptions are quiet **lava** flows that allow people plenty of time to get out of their way. These often cover large areas with lava.

Hot Spots in the Americas

In November 1985, one of the greatest natural disasters of the twentieth century took place high in the Andes Mountains of Colombia in South America. Here, in the Ring of Fire, the volcano Nevado del Ruiz erupted explosively. Blazing volcanic ash covered a nearby mountain valley. Suddenly an avalanche of mud swept down the valley and crashed into the farming town of Armero. The raging avalanche destroyed most of the town and swept away thousands of people in a steaming torrent of mud. Officials said that as many as 20,000 people in four valley towns died, and many more were left homeless.

El Salvador, in Central America, has twenty-two volcanoes that rise along the Ring of Fire. When the volcano Izalco erupts, lava covers the mountain from top to bottom. Salvadorans say that Izalco bathes itself in fire. El Salvador has three other active or recently active volcanoes. In this volcanic country, people are using some of their natural steam to produce electricity.

Mount St. Helens, in the state of Washington, is a well-known peak in the Ring of Fire. Its last major eruption was in May 1980. At that time the mountain's

In May 1980, an explosive eruption of Mount St. Helens blew the entire top off the mountain. (J. Rosenbaum)

entire top blew off and shot out on the north side. People and wildlife near Mount St. Helens were killed, and millions of fir trees were stripped and flattened like toothpicks. Even though this was a powerful eruption, it was a small one when compared with eruptions of other volcanoes in the Ring of Fire.

Asian Volcanoes

Across the Pacific Ocean from Mount St. Helens, Japan has about fifty volcanoes. Some "smoke," or vent steam and gases, most of the time. In 1914 an eruption of Sakurajima, a volcano on one of Japan's small volcanic islands, changed the island into a **peninsula**. When the area began to have strong earthquakes—warnings of a possible volcanic eruption—every available boat ferried people and their belongings to the mainland. Steamships joined in the rescue. In two days, everyone in the area was transported from the island. The people got away just in time. From the mainland, they watched the volcano explode and produce an enormous lava flow.

Mayon, a Ring-of-Fire volcano in the Philippines and one of the earth's most beautifully shaped volcanoes, erupts mildly most of the time. About every eleven years, though, Mayon has a more powerful eruption. Over the years this volcano has taken many lives through dust blasts. Floods and **mud slides** caused by its eruptions have washed people and property into the ocean.

Java, a small Indonesian island in the Ring of Fire, lies in one of the most volcanic parts of the world. At least thirty-five volcanoes fill this island. Some are active most of the time.

The people of Java continue to live near these dangerous, active volcanoes because they want to take advantage of the rich soil. Java has some of the world's most fertile soil—soil enriched by **ash** from volcanic eruptions. Within a few years after a volcanic ash dusting, the enriched land produces larger crops. The ash holds water within reach of new plants and rapidly releases plant food such as potassium.

Geysers and **hot springs** spring up all over Java. Long ago, the island's people learned many uses for them. They found that they could bathe and wash clothes in the hot springs where temperatures were not too great. In the hotter springs, by holding an attached cord and dangling a bag in the water, they cooked meat and vegetables.

Mayon, a Ring-of-Fire volcano in the Philippines, erupts powerfully about every eleven years. (J. G. Moore)

Underwater Eruptions

In addition to about five hundred active volcanoes located on land along the Ring of Fire, many volcanoes erupt from the ocean floor. They create effects similar to those created on land during volcanic eruptions.

An underwater volcano's outburst sends ocean life scurrying as water temperature increases and hot substances enter the ocean from the volcanic **vent**. After the eruption, remaining heat in the vent attracts ocean creatures that prefer warmer water.

Most of these underwater eruptions go unnoticed. Sometimes, though, a ship's crew notices violently boiling water or jets of water and steam erupting. Unless volcanoes build mountains that extend above the ocean's surface, most people never see them.

One mysterious island in the Ring of Fire is a "now-you-see-it, now-you-don't" island. Its name is Bogoslof. It is a 6,000-foot (1,525-meter) volcano rising from the ocean floor in the Aleutian Islands of Alaska. During the last 250 years, Bogoslof has been "discovered" several times. Each time it broke through the ocean surface and rose in a peak. Then, explosions from within the volcano and pounding waves from the ocean destroyed the volcanic peak. The island disappeared until another eruption lifted it, once more, above the water's surface.

Cracks in the Earth

Some of the world's most destructive earthquakes have taken place in the Ring of Fire. In 1933 the most powerful earthquake ever recorded sent shock waves across Japan's heartland. And in September 1985, a powerful earthquake in Mexico destroyed or damaged large areas of the world's largest city.

The earthquake was centered 250 miles (400 kilometers) southwest of Mexico City on Mexico's west coast—an area in the explosive Ring of Fire. Because much of Mexico City was built on an ancient lake bed of wet clay, many of its older buildings could not withstand the shaking of the earth. The earthquake destroyed or heavily damaged 450 buildings in the Mexican capital. At least 5,000 people died. After the earthquake, 50,000 volunteers worked desperately to save the people buried alive in the piles of rubble. Mexican President Miguel de la Madrid declared a national emergency in Mexico City and other hard-hit cities and towns. Once more the Ring of Fire had exploded in a way that people would long remember.

 # Why Do Volcanoes Erupt?

Most of the world's active volcanoes are found in two great belts. One follows the narrow, explosive band of the Ring of Fire. The other, the **Mediterranean Belt**, stretches from southern Europe to central Asia. Volcanoes occur in these small areas because of the make-up of the planet on which we live.

Scientists divide the earth into three main parts. The earth's surface, or **crust**, is three to five miles (five to eight kilometers) thick in the ocean basins and fifteen to thirty-five miles (twenty-five to fifty-eight kilometers) thick on the continents. It is made up of hard, rigid rock. Beneath the earth's crust is the 1,800-mile-thick (2,900-kilometer-thick) **mantle** that becomes hotter and more liquid toward the earth's center. Deeper parts of the mantle are semimolten—extremely hot and almost liquid. At the center of the earth is a very hot, solid ball known as the earth's **core**. The distance from the mantle to the earth's center is 2,200 miles (3,550 kilometers).

Plate Tectonics

Scientists believe that the outer parts of the earth move slowly over the inner ones. According to the science of **plate tectonics**, the earth's crust is like the cracked shell of a hard-boiled egg. It is broken into a number of sections called **plates**. Together, the crust and upper part of the mantle form six large plates and several smaller ones. These plates fit together and drift very slowly across the semimolten parts of the mantle beneath them. As they move, they carry along the continents and ocean basins.

In the mantle below these drifting plates, pressure is tremendous, and temperatures range from 1,600°F (870°C) to 4,000°F (2,200°C). Here, rocks and gases become a **molten** mass known as **magma**.

Until a crack or **fissure** opens in the rock above it, the magma remains quiet. Edges of crustal plates usually are the places where these cracks and fissures appear since the drifting plates collide along their edges. The plates grind against each other in constant motion and cause layers of rock on one or both plates to crack and break.

The Pacific Plate, on which most of the Pacific Ocean rides, collides with neighboring plates. Edges of one plate may move over the edges of another plate, causing it to bend downward into the mantle. This movement is called **subduction**.

Subduction causes earthquakes such as Mexico's in 1985. Often the violent shaking of the stronger earthquakes causes more rocks to crack and more fissures to open through miles of rock above.

Moving Magma

Now the magma has an escape route through these cracks and fissures. Far below the earth's surface, it begins to shift and rise into the crust. How far upward it moves depends on the pressure of the gases within it and on how far upward its channel extends.

Sometimes magma moves only partway through the earth's crust and creates a hot spot. At other times, though, cracks and fissures open a channel all the way to an ocean basin or to a land surface. Then magma pushes up through its channel, and a volcano erupts.

When magma erupts from a volcano, it is known as lava. There are different kinds of lava. Fluid lava spreads slowly down mountainsides. Tiny fragments of lava shot from a volcano harden as they meet the

Mount Merapi, on the island of Java in Indonesia, erupts in an area where one crustal plate is bending beneath another. (William P. Sterne, Jr.)

atmosphere. They are called volcanic ash. Pebble-sized pieces of airborne lava are known as **cinders**. As magma speeds up its channel to the earth's surface or to an ocean basin, it rips off hunks of rock and hurls them upward. These larger pieces of rock are called **bombs**.

Volcano Types

Volcanoes are divided into groups according to the way they act each time they erupt. If a volcano is erupting or shows signs of an eruption, we say that volcano is active. If a volcano has not erupted for a long time, then we say the volcano is **dormant**. If **volcanologists** (scientists who study volcanoes) believe a volcano will never erupt again, we say it is **extinct**. Sometimes, however, a volcano believed to be extinct suddenly begins to spew steam and other gases. Then we know it was not extinct, but was dormant and can become active again.

Volcanoes are also named according to their shapes. The most common kind of volcano is the **cinder cone**. Its shape is a steep-sided cone. It is built by ash, cinders, and bombs that pile up during an eruption. Cinder cones are formed by explosive eruptions.

In October 1980, on the last day of an eruption of the volcano Krafla, a fiery river of lava runs down the volcanic slopes. (H. Olafsson)

El Parícutin, a Mexican volcano, is a cinder cone.

Shield volcanoes are wide, gently-sloping mountains that are built up by lava from a pipelike hole or vent. Their eruptions are quiet lava flows. Kilauea, a volcano in the Hawaiian Islands, is a shield volcano.

Some volcanoes are called **composite volcanoes** because they have erupted in different ways at different times. These volcanoes are built in layers. During some eruptions, cinders, bombs, and blocks formed a mountain or added height to one that earlier volcanic eruptions had built. During other eruptions, lava flows cemented these rocks together. Mount St. Helens is a composite volcano.

The shape of a volcano tells us something about the chemicals and gases contained in the magma that created it. Magmas rich in **silica** are often found in very powerful eruptions. For example, Mount St. Helens's 1980 eruption contained large amounts of silica. Magmas rich in iron, magnesium, and calcium are less explosive. They are found mostly in fluid lava flows. In these eruptions, lava usually flows out over the rims of volcanic **craters** and from fissures in the sides of the mountains. Kilauea's eruptions are rich in iron, magnesium, and calcium.

Sometimes Mount St. Helens erupts explosively, as in this May 1980 eruption. At other times it erupts in quiet lava flows.

Warning Signs

In the Ring of Fire, earthquakes continue to shake and crack the earth as crustal plates push together and pull apart. Some scientists say that areas along the Ring of Fire should take steps to prevent or lessen the damage caused by earthquakes. In Mexico, for example, new buildings could be constructed so that they would withstand most earthquakes. Experts predict that the coastal area of California will be struck by a major earthquake by the year 2000. Recently, officials in that state have begun planning for such a disaster. Some older buildings and most new ones have been strengthened. Still, much remains to be done to prepare endangered areas for a major earthquake.

Earthquakes will create the right conditions for magma to move upward to the ocean bed or to land. In the future volcanoes such as Mount St. Helens will erupt as they have in the past. Some eruptions will be explosive, and others will be mild. Sometimes water from the oceans will fill great holes left by eruptions. Because of all this earth-shaking activity, the great belt around the edge of the Pacific Ocean will be known as the Ring of Fire for a very long time.

# An Eruption in a Cornfield

In February 1943, a Mexican farmer, Dionisio Publido, worked in his field hoeing the soil to get it ready for planting. He hoed the "low place," a small area six feet (nearly two meters) across that had sunk so that it was a little lower than other parts of the field. While the soil in most of his field was fertile, corn did not grow well in this spot. The farmer could not understand why. He gave this spot special attention.

Dionisio had no way of knowing that his village was part of the Ring of Fire. He did not know that his low place was a hot spot where magma had moved up through cracks and fissures. And he had no way of knowing that heat from the magma kept corn from growing well in this part of his field.

Fire in the Earth

Suddenly, as he watched, wisps of a smokelike vapor rose out of a crack in the low place. When the ground beneath his feet began to shake, he could hardly stand up. Dionisio had felt rumbling and shaking many times during the past two weeks. The strange movement had rattled dishes and cracked his house's plaster walls. This time the rumbling was louder, and the shaking was stronger.

The rumbling and shaking had been warnings. Soon they were followed by earth movements known as **harmonic tremors**. Volcanologists believe harmonic tremors are a sign that molten magma is moving upward from deep within the earth. When magma rises, a volcano can erupt at any time. Large amounts of gases trapped within magma may cause a volcano to erupt with great explosive force.

Dionisio retreated as steam and dark clouds of ash rose higher and higher from the low place. In their midst fire flashed and crackled, and then he heard a series of explosions. A fountain of brilliant red rocks and ash erupted high into the air. Some rocks were the size of his fist; others were as large as his one-room house. As the deafening explosions became stronger, rocks shot higher, and heavy black clouds of ash filled the sky. A red glow hung above the ground. The strong smell of rotten eggs came from the sulfurous fumes that poured out of the volcano.

Paricutin erupting in what was once a Mexican cornfield tilled by Dionisio Publido and his family. (R.E. Wilcox)

A Frightened Family

Dionisio and his family were horrified. They thought that these strange happenings must be caused by an evil creature inside the earth. As they hurried through the streets, the frightened family talked loudly with other residents of the village of Parícutin and tried to decide what to do. They did not realize that what they watched was a volcanic eruption.

Finally, Dionisio ran all the way to San Juan—a town three miles (five kilometers) away—to tell the people there what was happening. By the time he reached San Juan, the big clouds of ash with fire at the base were visible there, too. Soon he raced back to Parícutin.

As many other people living in the Ring of Fire have done, Dionisio's family prepared to leave their home. They began loading their possessions—blankets, food, and kitchen utensils—on the back of their burro. Other villagers, too, packed their belongings on their burros and started traveling toward San Juan.

All through the night, from a nearby hillside, people of the village of Parícutin watched as the eruptions continued. The big rock pile that had been Dionisio's cornfield was circled with fire. Its center was a red torch. By morning the cornfield was covered with a 200-foot-tall (61-meter-tall) mountain of black rocks.

The Birth of a Volcano

It was a small volcano. Some volcanoes never become larger than this one, while others rise to take their place among the taller mountains of the world.

Rocks continued to shoot from the volcano and fall back onto the newly-formed mountain. Higher and higher it grew. The center of the volcano acted as a chimney for rocks, steam, and ashes to escape.

Day after day, explosions and fireworks continued. Dionisio, his family and many of their neighbors returned to their homes. They decided that, for now, they would just stay out of the path of those hot rocks and hope that the terrible fireworks would stop.

Everything within five miles (eight kilometers) of the volcano was covered with a foot or more of volcanic ash. Two hundred miles (three hundred twenty kilometers) away in Mexico City, ash from this faraway, fiery mountain fell on rooftops and in the streets.

A week later, lava began to gush and shoot outward like jets of water from the sides of the volcano. It

A huge lava bed buried what was once the village of Parícutin. Later it covered the nearby town of San Juan, too. (K. Segerstrom)

looked like darkened bread dough streaked with fire. It flowed slowly down the sides of the volcano, digging its way through the ash. Each time one flow stopped, another broke out nearby. Finally, it covered much of the land below.

Dionisio and his family became more and more frightened as the lava approached their home. Gritty ash from the volcano piled up on their roof faster than they could clean it off. Ash blocked the streets and seeped into houses. Since they knew it was no longer safe to stay, they packed their belongings on their burro again and left. All of the people in the village of Parícutin left their homes, too. This time they did not return.

The red-hot lava showed no signs of stopping. For months a million tons poured out of the volcano each day. Volcanologists came to Parícutin from many countries. They wanted to witness the birth of a volcano. For them it was the experience of a lifetime.

To measure the strength of the eruptions, the scientists placed instruments on nearby mountaintops. They measured the lava flow and checked its temperature.

Leaving Home

The volcano kept on erupting until Dionisio's entire village was buried. Later, the people of San Juan also had to leave their homes. Lava continued to flow until it buried their town, too.

The volcano, El Parícutin—named for the first village it buried—erupted for nine years before it became quiet. Every tree and plant for twenty miles

Four years after Parícutin's first eruption, a scientist stands by equipment he has prepared to conduct tests near the volcano. (K. Segerstrom)

(thirty-two kilometers) in all directions had been destroyed. More than 8,000 people had fled from their homes. A huge lava bed had been created. Many years would pass before this land could be farmed again.

No lives were lost as a result of El Parícutin's eruption. People in the village of Parícutin and in San Juan had time to pack their belongings and to get out of the volcano's path.

The eruption of El Parícutin provided volcanologists with a great deal of information. Around the world it created much interest in the study of volcanoes. People everywhere became more aware of the enormous power of volcanoes and the far-reaching effects of their eruptions.

4 An Island Blown Apart

One of the greatest natural explosions ever recorded took place at Krakatoa, a small volcanic island in the Ring of Fire. This volcano is in Indonesia, to the northwest of Australia in the western Pacific Ocean. In 1883 it was a land of lush tropical forests.

Krakatoa and its neighboring volcanic islands had been created millions of years ago. Magma had pushed up into the Pacific Ocean bed and built underwater mountains, or **seamounts**, higher and higher. All the while, the weight of the ocean water pushed down on these growing mountains. Finally, the volcanic peaks broke the ocean's surface as islands.

Volcanic eruptions often occurred here because Krakatoa rises at the point where two fissures meet in the **Sundra Strait**. Here, one crustal plate is slowly sliding beneath another plate. As it moves, its edge is being subducted into the earth's mantle.

On either side of Krakatoa along the same edge of this crustal plate are the islands of Java and Sumatra.

A submarine eruption explodes through the surface of the Pacific Ocean. Krakatoa and neighboring islands were created millions of years ago by such eruptions.

Unlike Krakatoa, many people live on these two larger islands.

Warning Signs

In May 1883, a volcano on the island of Krakatoa began to show early signs of an eruption. Rumblings that sounded like gunfire rattled windows in Java and Sumatra. The crew of a boat sailing in the Sundra Strait noticed the ship's compass needle shifting back and forth rapidly. Earthquakes were shaking the strait and the islands.

People in Java and Sumatra ignored the rumblings. They went about their usual activities, which centered around the ships in this important sea lane.

On the next day, a black vapor rose in the air from the volcano's base. The volcano sputtered more and more. Still, people on neighboring islands felt safe.

Then, lightning flashed in the vapor that shot up higher than five miles (eight kilometers) into the sky. The air smelled of sulfur. Explosions grew louder and louder. Ash and **pumice** from the volcano coated the islands and ships sailing in the Sundra Strait.

About the time people in Java and Sumatra began to worry about their safety, Krakatoa seemed to calm down. They thought that the time of greatest danger had passed. An exploration party from Java even landed on the island to inspect the damage.

For several weeks Krakatoa erupted mildly. Although nobody was aware of it, the volcano was building up pressure inside. Seawater may have seeped into the crater through a crack in its volcanic cone. Scientists believe that cool water may have caused the top part of the cone to harden and form a plug. The plug at the top would have forced a sudden build-up of heat and pressure deep within the volcano.

The Great Eruption

On August 26 and 27 a series of deafening explosions shot ash seventeen miles (twenty-eight kilometers) into the sky and caused two-thirds of the island to disappear. The eruption blew more than five cubic miles of pumice and other hot rock out of its chimney. It created a huge bowl-shaped pit, or **caldera**, five miles (eight kilometers) across. Part of Krakatoa's cone had collapsed, or fallen, into the magma chamber.

Where land had once been, the ocean now filled holes 100 feet (30.5 meters) deep. Flying rocks and ash shut off sunlight for 150 miles (240 kilometers) from the eruption. Thick fields of pumice thrown out by the volcano floated on the ocean's surface for many miles in islandlike shapes.

More than 1,300 miles (2,100 kilometers) from Krakatoa, people heard the explosion and thought the sounds came from a ship in distress. They sent boats

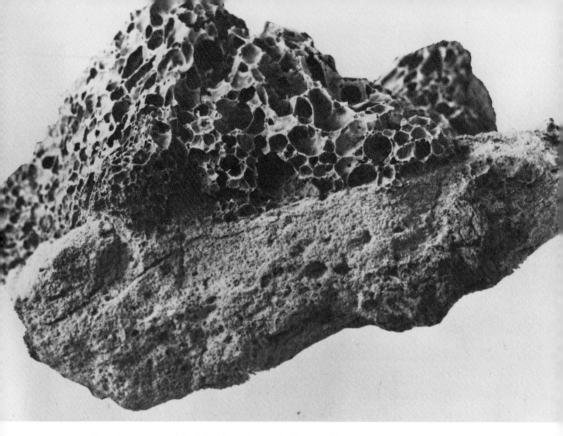

Pumice—a very light volcanic rock filled with tiny gas bubbles—floated in thick fields, or "islands," in the sea around Krakatoa. This piece of pumice is attached to a heavier piece of rock. (H. T. Stearns)

to the rescue. At a distance of 3,000 miles (5,000 kilometers), people heard the explosion and thought it was faraway gunfire.

The volcanic ash, mixed with moisture in the air, rained down as mud on boat decks and rigging. Layers of muddy ash made the boats slick and top-heavy.

Finally, the worst seemed to be over. Actually, it was just beginning.

Deadly Waves From the Sea

Part of the energy from Krakatoa's explosion transferred to the surrounding ocean. It created **tsunamis**—extremely large, long and deadly waves. These moved out from Krakatoa toward the islands of Java and Sumatra.

At great depth, tsunamis may travel at several hundred miles an hour. As they near the shore, friction from the shallow bottom causes them to slow down. As each wave moves closer to the next, giant sea waves rise up out of the water.

When the tsunamis reached Java and Sumatra, the waves were nearly 130 feet (40 meters) high. Wave after giant wave swept over the shores of these islands.

When the tsunamis struck, towns near the shores of Java and Sumatra were buzzing with activity. People were buying, selling, and doing business as usual. Caught without warning, many were swept away into the ocean and drowned.

The high, speeding waves destroyed 295 towns on the islands of Java and Sumatra. Ships passing through the straits were smashed to bits. A Dutch warship was washed ashore and stranded half a mile inland, thirty feet (nine meters) above sea level. Buildings fifty feet (fifteen meters) above sea level were washed into the ocean.

No one knows exactly how many lives the ocean claimed that day on the islands and in the straits. More than 36,000 people died.

While ships in the straits were torn apart by the tsunamis, one ship farther out in the ocean survived the big waves. The ship's captain decided to meet the waves head-on and attempt to ride over them. It was a dangerous ride, but the crew survived to tell about it.

A Global Event

As news of this terrible disaster spread around the world, people reacted with stunned disbelief. Most could not imagine a natural disaster of such great power that could affect people so far away.

Clouds of floating dust from Krakatoa's eruption spread into the upper part of the earth's atmosphere. Winds carried ash for great distances. The dusty ash in the sky gave people all over the world brilliant red sunrises and sunsets for the next year.

Pumice from the eruption covered the water around Krakatoa. Pumice is a rock filled with tiny gas

Volcanologists study volcanoes such as Hekla in Iceland (above) *to learn more about how eruptions occur. In the future they hope to be able to predict dangerous eruptions like the one on Krakatoa so that people can be warned in advance.*

bubbles that is so lightweight it will float. The floating rock was carried by ocean currents for thousands of miles in the seven months following the eruption. Some of it probably floated around the globe.

During the past hundred years, Krakatoa has erupted only mildly. Will this volcano in the Ring of Fire someday erupt violently again? We do not know, but volcanologists are trying hard to find the answer.

 # The Hot Spot

Located in the mid-Pacific Ocean, the Hawaiian Islands are not in the Ring of Fire but are surrounded by it. These beautiful and peaceful-looking islands are the result of millions of years of action between fire and water. They were not formed, as volcanoes in the Ring of Fire, when edges of plates pushed together and opened up channels to the earth's surface. Instead, this inside part of the Pacific Plate sits on a hot spot, or **plume**. From this fixed hot spot, magma breaks out from time to time through the ocean floor. The Pacific Plate moves across the mid-ocean plume in a northwesterly direction at a rate of three to five inches (eight to thirteen centimeters) each year.

Islands in the Sea

Volcanologists believe the entire chain of Hawaiian Islands was formed as volcanoes erupted from the Pacific Ocean floor above this plume. Millions of years ago, they believe, volcanoes created the north-

ernmost island. Volcanic eruptions built up an underwater mountain, higher and higher, from the ocean
floor. At last this mountain rose above the ocean's
surface to become an island. Lava from later eruptions flowed to the ocean, adding more land and making the island wider and longer. Each eruption added
height to the island.

After millions of years, waves and weather wore
down the volcanic rock. Now people began to live on
the island and use the soil for farmland. Plants and
animals had come to the island even earlier. Creatures that preferred high elevations lived near the
mountain's summit. Others lived farther down the
mountainside.

Birds found volcanic nest-building material in the
form of lightweight, thread-sized strands that look
like spun glass. These strands, known as "Pelee's
hair," sometimes are formed as steam passes through
a mass of molten lava. Pelee's hair often collects on
cliffs or in trees after volcanic eruptions.

As the Pacific Plate moved northwestward, the
northernmost island of the Hawaiian Islands moved
off the hot spot. As it moved, its "plumbing" was
removed from the source of magma. When magma

Kilauea, a famous Hawaiian volcano, erupting in 1974. Lava from volcanoes such as this one built up the Hawaiian Islands from the ocean floor thousands of feet beneath the surface. (D.W. Peterson)

within this volcano was used up, its volcanic activity and its growth stopped. The volcano that had built the island became extinct.

Meanwhile, other volcanoes erupted in the ocean. Gradually, they built another island southeast of the first one in the new area that was now located over the hot spot.

For millions of years, this process continued. Today, the 2,000-mile-long (3,200-kilometer-long) chain of islands that we call Hawaii includes eight large islands and many small ones.

Fire and Water

Volcanoes erupting in the ocean meet with more resistance than those erupting on land. If you ever swam in the ocean, you felt the power of the water. This power, aided by storms, has sent mighty ships to the bottom. Yet, the force of an erupting volcano is so great that it shoots up in spite of the weight of the ocean.

At a volcano's first eruption from the ocean floor, the struggle between powerful opposing forces begins. In the region of the Hawaiian Islands, water is 16,000 feet (4,880 meters) deep. The tremendous

weight of the water at this depth presses down on the
newly formed volcano. As the mountain is built up by
later eruptions, the struggle between fire and water
continues. When the mountain breaks the ocean's surface and becomes an island, ocean waves pound at its
edges. Aided by wind and storms, they **erode** and
wash away soft parts of the mountain, carving cliffs
and caves. The building up and breaking down ac-
tions go on and on.

As the volcanoes that built each island became
extinct, the building stopped. Yet the ocean continued
to erode the island's beaches. Other volcanoes, new
and old, built up more islands in the Hawaiian chain.

Solving a Mystery

As volcanologists studied the Hawaiian Islands,
one problem bothered them. They knew that when
molten lava meets ocean water and is suddenly
cooled, often it shatters into tiny pieces. How, then,
could underwater volcanoes build up? They would be
cooled immediately by ocean water during their entire formation.

Divers found the answer to this puzzle when they
photographed underwater eruptions of a Hawaiian

volcano. Amid roaring noises, lava shot out from a **fracture line** in the underwater portion of the volcano. Within two or three seconds, the lava had cooled and formed an extension, or **pillow**, on the underwater mountain. The divers continued filming as this same erupting and cooling process was repeated again and again along the fracture line. Sometimes a pillow would crack open, and another pillow would form at the crack.

Volcanologists knew that lava tubes form on land as the outside of the lava flow hardens. Inside the tube, lava is still flowing. Finally, all of the lava flows on, leaving a hollow tube.

The scientists realized that divers had filmed a similar scene in the ocean. Water cools the outside of a lava flow while molten lava still flows inside. The molten lava breaks out again and again, forming pillows. Their outsides harden, allowing the lava inside to keep flowing and breaking out steadily. As this underwater action continues, the volcano rises through the ocean depths.

The divers were thrilled with their discovery. Filming as rapidly as possible, they wasted no time in getting out of the way of this erupting volcano.

The Thurston lava tube was formed on land as the outside of a lava tube hardened. Volcanoes in the ocean build by forming hollow "pillows" from erupting lava.

Eruptions of volcanoes in the Hawaiian Islands are much less violent than those of Parícutin, Krakatoa, and others in the Ring of Fire. Hawaiian volcanoes usually erupt before explosive pressures build up. Their eruptions spew fiery lava into the air from long fissures. Then lava cascades down the mountainsides and sometimes pushes to the ocean. In this way, more land is created. Ocean waves pound the island's

A fiery river of lava runs down the slope of an erupting volcano.

shores, gradually breaking volcanic rock down to create sand beaches.

Passing Over the Plume

Volcanoes on islands northwest of the island of Hawaii are now extinct. They have passed completely over the hot plume on the ocean floor. The island of Hawaii, the largest of the Hawaiian Islands, is now passing over the hot spot. Volcanoes are still building this island as it moves slowly northwestward.

Only two volcanoes in the Hawaiian Islands, Kilauea and its neighbor, Mauna Loa, are still active. Both are young volcanoes. Kilauea is older, but Mauna Loa is larger. Once they stood as two separate volcanoes. Now, although the summits of the two mountains are twenty-two miles (thirty-five kilometers) apart, lava flows from vents of both volcanoes have filled the valleys between them. Kilauea no longer looks like a mountain. Its summit has collapsed and formed a cup-shaped hole on the southeastern slope of Mauna Loa. The 400-foot-deep (122-meter-deep) hole is Kilauea's crater—in this case a caldera.

We do not know how much larger these volcanoes will become, but one mountain on this island is a real giant. Mauna Kea, an extinct volcano, rises 14,000 feet (4,270 meters) above sea level. Yet this is less than half its real size. Long ago it erupted from the ocean floor and rose to 16,000 feet (4,880 meters) before it reached the ocean's surface. Measuring from the ocean floor, then, its total height is 30,000 feet (9,150 meters).

Thirty miles (forty-eight kilometers) southeast of the island of Hawaii, another mountain is now located over the hot spot. Named Loihi, this volcano's peak still is 3,000 feet (945 meters) below the ocean's surface. If the struggle between fire and water that is building this new mountain continues, Loihi may someday become another island in the Hawaiian chain.

Visitors to the Hawaiian Islands enjoy the results of the volcanic action that created these islands. Some of the world's finest scenery is found here. Created by oceans and volcanoes, it remains to enrich the lives of future generations.

6 Fire Fountains and Spouting Lava

Kilauea, a volcano on the island of Hawaii, is sometimes called the "drive-in" volcano. When Kilauea erupts, visitors rush toward it to watch its fireworks. Often during an eruption, automobiles clog the highway leading to Kilauea's crater rim. As the people arrive, rangers usher them to safe places where they have a good view of the volcano's eruption.

Kilauea, one of the world's most active volcanoes, entertains them with a giant display of **fire fountains** and spouting lava. The lava pours down the mountainside in fiery, oozing rivers. People who have watched these powerful fireworks never forget the glowing, exploding lava. They remember, too, the rumbling sounds, the shaking of the ground, and the feeling of awe in the presence of nature's fury.

A Mild-Mannered Volcano

Unlike volcanoes such as Krakatoa that erupt explosively, Kilauea's fluid lava lets gases escape before

An arching fire fountain from Kilauea entertains visitors to the "drive in" Hawaiian volcano. (J.D. Griggs)

they build up great pressure. As a result, Kilauea usually has mild-mannered eruptions. Most of the time, after magma fills a reservoir beneath the volcano's summit, enormous amounts of fluid lava erupt from vents and fissures. These red-hot lava flows often move down the mountainside twenty miles (thirty-two kilometers) or more before they cool and harden.

In 1959, a fire fountain from an eruption on Kilauea reached 1,900 feet (600 meters) in height. As this remarkable eruption continued, it buried a village, flowed to the ocean, and added 500 acres of land to the island of Hawaii. This volcano, like most other volcanoes, had destroyed some areas and built up others.

"The House of Everlasting Fire"

Beginning in 1969, Kilauea erupted for two and one-half years. During this time thousands of visitors drove up to the crater rim to see the drive-in volcano in action. In a way they experienced an ancient Hawaiian legend.

Within Kilauea's large caldera is a smaller crater named Halemaumau, meaning "The House of Everlasting Fire." A legend says that this is the home of Pele, the Polynesian volcano goddess. When Pele digs with

In the foreground, lava erupts on the floor of Kilauea's caldera. In the background, smoke rises from Halemaumau, the legendary crater.

her magic stick, according to the legend, flames rise from the volcano.

In the past Halemaumau contained a lake of boiling lava with temperatures greater than 2,000°F (1,093°C). At times this lake rose and fell. Now, the crater looks like a giant bowl of pudding that still shows pocks and rings from its bubbling. Many eruptions occur within this deep pit, which is Kilauea's main vent. Lava flows from Halemaumau often spill over into the larger crater. Other eruptions break out in fissures.

Studying Volcanoes

The Hawaiian Volcano Observatory and research laboratory perches on the rim of Kilauea's crater. This is the finest and best equipped volcano observatory on earth. Its instruments are so delicately balanced that they can record the pressure of footsteps on a cement floor. Here, volcanologists can gather valuable information about volcanoes with little risk to their own safety.

Kilauea helps them "see" into the earth's interior. The scientists study ash, cinders, and bombs that first formed inside the earth as magma. They observe Kilauea's lava flows. Through this volcano, they learn about the earth's depths.

Our deepest oil wells drill just a short distance into the earth's crust in the ocean and on land. Knowledge gained from them adds to our understanding of the crust. By observing Kilauea, though, volcanolo-

Scientists at the Hawaiian Volcano Observatory and research laboratory gather valuable information about volcanoes.

gists learn about the makeup of the earth's mantle.

From studies at this observatory, scientists are also learning more about what to expect from volcanoes. Often, they are able to predict correctly the time of an eruption of Kilauea.

Volcanologists here wondered if they could take action to change the direction of a volcano's lava flow. Hawaii's volcanoes allow time for people to escape

Designed and built by the Hawaiian Volcano Observatory, this semi-portable tiltmeter measures mountain swelling. Instruments at the observatory are so delicately balanced that they can record the pressure of footsteps on a cement floor. Since Kilauea poses little danger to nearby observers, the observatory was built almost at the rim of Kilauea's crater. (R.H. Finch)

from their eruptions. Still, when a lava flow covers a city, property damage is high. The scientists tried bombing lava flows in an attempt to change their directions. They tried building barricades to force lava rivers to change their courses. Both methods showed that they could be used to help prevent property damage during an eruption.

Because Kilauea is less explosive than most volcanoes, it is safer to study. Since 1911, activities of this volcano have been continuously recorded. At the Hawaiian Volcano Observatory, **seismographs** record earthquakes in Hawaii and in the Ring of Fire. **Tiltmeters** measure mountain swelling.

Before an eruption, underground pressure causes Kilauea's **dome** to swell like a balloon filling with air. Sometimes its summit rises several feet higher than normal. When strong shaking from an earthquake comes at the same time as this swollen dome suddenly falls back down, volcanologists give an eruption warning. Kilauea is ready to entertain visitors again with its fireworks!

7 Land of Fire and Frost

In the Atlantic Ocean, far from the Hawaiian Islands and Ring of Fire, the earth's moving plates caused a series of islands to be formed. Iceland sits on top of the Atlantic Ridge, part of a 40,000-mile-long (64,000-kilometer-long) volcanic mountain range on the ocean floor. This mountain range winds through the world's oceans in places where crustal plates are spreading. Where magma pushes upward and forces the plates apart, ridges form on the ocean floor. This movement is called **sea-floor spreading**.

Eruption after eruption builds these volcanoes higher in spite of the weight of ocean water above them. They are so large and heavy that sometimes they cause parts of the ocean bed beneath them to collapse.

Iceland is one of four places where this mountain range has formed islands. Magma pushed up between the North American and Eurasian plates millions of years ago, forcing the plates apart. As eruptions con-

In Iceland volcanic craters are a common sight.

tinued, these underwater mountains finally built high enough to reach the ocean's surface.

As in the Hawaiian Islands, Iceland's mountain building was a constant struggle between fire and water. Here, too, ocean waves, wind, and storms have carved the island's coastline.

A Volcanic Wonderland

Today, parts of Iceland are 7,000 feet (2,130 meters) above sea level. Volcanoes are lined up across the center of the island in a northeasterly-southwesterly direction. They rise directly above the place where the North American and Eurasian plates have been pushed apart by sea-floor spreading.

Iceland is one of the most volcanic areas on earth. During the last 500 years, one-third of the lava that erupted from volcanoes all over the world erupted in Iceland.

In Iceland, also, reservoirs of magma heat underground rivers of water which surface as geysers and hot springs. Iceland has at least thirty geysers and hundreds of hot springs.

It takes thousands of years for magma to cool. Meanwhile, rainwater and melted snow seep down

A jet shoots out from a tiny lava pool in Iceland. Iceland is one of the most volcanic areas on earth. (S. Thorarinsson)

through cracks in the rock below. There they circulate for miles underground. When this water reaches rocks that are heated by pockets of magma, it becomes extremely hot. Eventually, when great pressure has built up in the hot water, it rises to the earth's surface through small cracks or tubes.

Since Iceland sits on the ridge where the ocean is spreading, Iceland, too, is spreading at about an inch each year. This spreading causes **rifts** that run in a northeasterly-southwesterly direction across the country. Volcanic explosions occur along these rifts, shooting out lava that covers large areas of the countryside. Iceland continues to grow from sea-floor spreading and from volcanic eruptions that build the island higher, wider, and longer.

Glaciers and lava deserts cover much of Iceland. When a volcano erupts underneath a glacier, a deadly combination of fiery lava and water destroys everything in its path. Geysers and hot springs underneath a glacier also cause melting and flooding.

Living with Volcanoes

Some hotels in Iceland post civil defense warnings. The warnings explain what to do if sirens sound alternately high and low tones while red rockets are being fired.

This alarm signals an eruption from the volcano Krafla. Here, fissures opened up and lava shot out six times between 1975 and 1980. At times Krafla has caused people living nearby to keep their suitcases packed. They needed to be ready to leave their homes at once if Krafla erupted suddenly.

While this warning may frighten visitors, Icelanders have learned to cope with the natural violence of their country. Most Icelanders are calm, brave, and determined to do whatever has to be done. They expect an eruption from one or more of their volcanoes every five years. In 1980, the volcanoes Krafla and Hekla were active at the same time.

Mount Hekla is the most famous volcano in Iceland. Long ago, people thought it was the main gateway to hell. This volcano has had twenty severe eruptions since written records have been kept. Once it continued erupting for six years.

Two hundred years ago in Iceland, eruptions from the volcano Skaptar Jökull caused a great disaster. Heat from fiery lava suddenly melted snow and glaciers on the mountain. By the time the eruptions

During an October 1980 eruption, fiery lava flows pour down the slopes of the Icelandic volcano Krafla. (Pall Imsland)

ended, they had killed one-fifth of Iceland's people and more than half of the cattle, sheep, and horses.

Helgafell is another famous Icelandic volcano. Its eruptions created Heimaey, one of the Westmann Islands south of the main island.

In 1973, Helgafell's eruption threatened to block the entrance to Iceland's biggest fishing port. Most people on Heimaey fled to the mainland. Those who remained behind knew that if the volcano closed the port, their means of earning a living would be gone. They decided to try something new in an attempt to save their harbor.

Ocean water surrounded the island. The people of Heimaey wondered what would happen if they sprayed it on the front of the river of lava. Would it cool and harden the lava enough to stop its flow? They decided that this plan was worth trying.

Pumps and hoses were flown in and put in place. Fed with seawater by dredging boats, the hoses sprayed 29,000 tons of water an hour on the fiery lava. For five months, the island's people kept fighting the volcanic river. The cold water hardened the outside of the flow, sometimes stopping it. At times lava broke through in a new place. Then the determined lava

On Heimaey in January 1973, Icelanders hurry to pack up furniture to save it from the advancing lava flowing from Helgafell.

fighters sprayed water to stop the flow again.

Although the hot lava destroyed many homes in the town and buried part of the land under a towering lava wall, the harbor was saved. A month after the volcano stopped erupting, people began to return to the island. Workers built new roads, houses, and a hospital to replace those buried by the volcano. To form the foundations for the buildings and roads, they used basalt. It is a very hard and sturdy rock that was thrown out by the volcano onto Heimaey.

Energy from the Earth

Icelanders are also taking advantage of the natural hot water and steam from their geysers and hot springs. This water is boiling or near boiling when it reaches the earth's surface. It is used just as it comes from the ground to fill and heat nearly a hundred bathing pools in Iceland. As a result, people in Iceland can enjoy open air swimming both in summer and winter.

One-fourth of Iceland's homes are also heated by natural hot water. In the homes it is used for cooking and laundry.

Icelanders discovered that after natural hot water has been used to heat houses, it still is warm enough to heat greenhouses. Many flowers are raised in Iceland's greenhouses using this warm water.

In recent years Iceland's people have used steam from high-pressure wells to produce electricity. Most electricity is made by burning gas, oil, and coal to heat steam. When people use the energy from natural steam to turn **turbines**, they save gas, oil, or coal that would have been used in its place. Natural steam also is cleaner and less costly to use than these **fossil fuels**.

Oceanographers and volcanologists delight in studying Iceland. In other parts of the world, they must go to the ocean floor in order to learn what is happening there. In Iceland, they can hike along the island and measure the growing rift between North America and Europe. With the help of tiltmeters, **rift-meters** and seismographs, they can predict weeks in advance that an eruption will occur. Then Icelanders can leave their homes or take steps to protect lives and property.

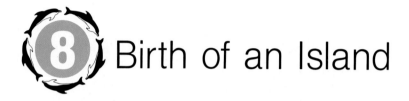 # 8 Birth of an Island

Volcanologists believe that Iceland formed long ago in much the same way as a new island formed off its southern coast. On November 14, 1963, a rumble rose from the ocean south of Iceland. As it grew louder, one spot bubbled, and the smell of sulfur filled the air. Dark circles moved in the water.

Puffins, birds that normally fly and fish near the water's surface, fled. Even gulls left the area.

As the rumbling grew louder, a circle of water seemed to be sucked downward, leaving a hole. From it, a bubble of ash burst and scattered, then fell back into the water. A volcano was erupting in the ocean!

The crew of a fishing vessel watched the ash shoot out from one vent, and then from two separate vents. Columns of black vapor rose in the air just above the water's surface. Soon they shot up higher and higher. The volcano hurled bombs, cinders, and ash that sometimes blazed with lightning flashes. Finally, the eruption column reached a height of more

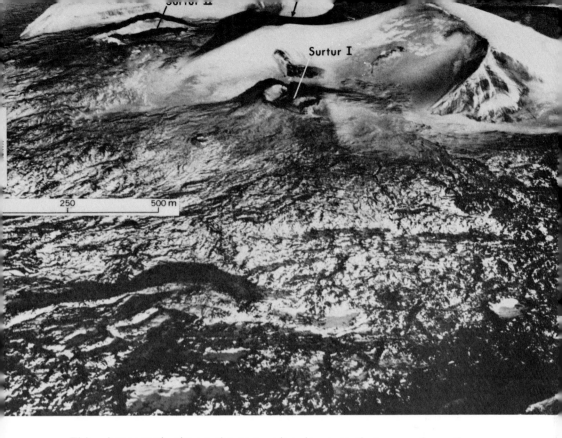

Surtur I

250   500 m

This photograph shows the two volcanic vents that rose above the ocean's surface to form the island of Surtsey in November 1963. (J.D. Friedman)

than four miles (about six kilometers). At night it glowed with a pinkish hue. The ocean turned brownish-green near the eruption. Hot ash and bombs sizzled as they fell into the water.

The Birth of an Island

Now a ridge developed just above the water's surface along the line that marks the edges of the

North American and Eurasian plates. A new island was being born. It was a cinder cone volcano.

The struggle between fire and water had begun 425 feet (130 meters) below the water's surface at the ocean floor. Now it continued at the surface. With tremendous force, rocks, boulders, and ash shot into the air and landed on top of the stones thrown out by earlier eruptions. But the ocean, ever moving with great force, pounded the light, newly-formed rocks. It began eroding them as they fell. Each new wave rolled and scattered the lighter rock pieces. Bombs sizzled as they touched ocean water and turned it into steam. Ash washed off the island and scattered in the ocean.

For four and a half months, the volcano erupted from one or both vents. Eruptions built land, and the ocean erased or reshaped it. Large waves lashed at the island's cliffs. The volcanic vents were named Surter I and Surter II, and the island they created was named Surtsey.

Earth had a new island, but could it withstand the fury of the ocean? If not, its air-filled cinder pile would be washed away.

As the volcano rose above the sea, a glowing lava lake built higher and higher in its vent. The lava

An aerial view of Surtsey shows lava from a volcanic vent running down to the sea where the hot lava produces a huge cloud of steam.

spilled over the sides and flowed in narrow, fiery streams down the mountainside. These streams divided into more tiny streams. As each reached the ocean, the water reacted to the fiery lava by producing huge clouds of steam. Floating pumice covered large patches of water.

The battle raged on. Each fiery lava flow helped to cement the rocks together, coat the island with lava, and form a shell. Then, for a while, the lava flows stopped.

Six months later, the lava flowed again. This time it continued for seven months, coating the island with a hard shell. Surtsey was here to stay. The ocean, too, had helped make the island sturdy. Waves had broken away the weakest parts as the island was built.

Surtsey was now 573 feet (172 meters) high and had an area of 1 square mile (2.5 square kilometers). Yet, only 9 percent of the volcanic material that formed Surtsey is visible. The other 91 percent is the base that built up underwater and now supports the island.

Two more eruptions occurred in the same area of the ocean while Surtsey was building. In both cases the ocean washed away the struggling, would-be islands.

Life on Surtsey

Now that Surtsey's fires had ceased, the island began to cool. At first, its surface had no form of life. Gradually, it became the home of plants and animals.

On Surtsey in the fall of 1965, newly erupted lava flows over older, ash-covered lava.

Again, the ocean played a part. It scattered boulders on the leeward side (side the wind blows toward) of the island. Behind these large rocks, seeds were somewhat protected.

Gulls investigated the island while it was still warm. Their droppings contained weed seeds. Ocean waves washed in other seeds. A few found a place on this new island where they could put down roots. Mosses followed. Carried in by the wind, their spores clung to cracks in the rocks.

Gradually, migrating birds began to rest on the island's cliffs and drink from its **lagoon**. Puffins came to fish off its shores. Within a year, an occasional seal napped on the black sand beach.

A year and a half after its birth, Surtsey was declared a sanctuary, or protected place. Scientists arrived to study its development. A small house was built for them to use—the only building on the island. Scientists follow strict rules on Surtsey. They are allowed to watch and record its development, but are not allowed to harm or help any plant or animal.

Biologists—scientists who study plants and animals—watched a sturdy plant called the sea rocket flower and set fruit. It was the first plant to do so on the island. Its delicate green leaves stood out against the barren black rocks of the volcanic mountain.

By observing the island of Surtsey, volcanologists hope to learn more about volcanoes—particularly the volcanoes that formed Iceland. Oceanographers are learning what part the ocean plays in shaping and building new islands.

Scientists do not know what will happen to Surtsey's volcanic vents in the future. They do know that ocean waves will continue to erode Surtsey's beach. If other eruptions occur, the ocean will again play its part in making the new part of the island sturdy.

The ocean is aiding Surtsey in yet another way. The **Gulf Stream**—a warm river in the ocean that circles past this island—carries warm water from the tropics. This warmth helps create a somewhat mild climate on this new island in the North Atlantic Ocean.

9 What Can We Do?

Scientists cannot stop volcanoes from erupting nor earthquakes from shaking nor great sea waves from rushing to land. They can, however, continue to study these natural events so that they can better predict when they will occur. If warnings are given well in advance of a volcanic eruption or earthquake, people will have enough time to leave dangerous areas and protect their property.

Scientists, too, can keep looking for ways to "manage" what they cannot stop. For example, they may discover better ways to change the direction of a lava flow when it is moving toward a place where people live. They may also find more ways to use valuable minerals brought up from the earth's mantle by erupting volcanoes.

Oceanographers, **geologists**, and volcanologists around the world are piecing together bits of new information about oceans and volcanic activity. These scientists are trying to learn how to make use of

Volcanologists use instruments such as this seismometer to determine what is happening deep within the earth's crust.

nature's energy in order to help people everywhere.

Some forms of nature's energy are already being used by humans. Natural hot water from hot springs and geysers heats homes and provides recreation in some countries. Natural underground steam also has practical uses. Its temperatures are hotter than the temperatures of natural hot water. Scientists are looking for ways in which natural steam can help solve world energy problems.

Geothermal Power

Electricity produced by natural steam is called **geothermal power**. It is now being used in several places around the world that have natural steam. In the Ring of Fire, El Salvador, Mexico, Japan, and Indonesia make use of this source of power. In New Zealand, natural steam produces electricity at a much lower cost than electric power produced by using fossil fuels.

Another place in the Ring of Fire that uses natural steam is the Geysers in northern California. This is an area of dying volcanic activity, where a pocket of magma still heats rocks for miles around it. Here, water moving 1,000 feet (305 meters) below the

This geothermal power station in El Salvador produces electricity by using natural steam to turn turbines. (Don Yager)

earth's surface is heated by these rocks to 375° F (191°C). When this superheated water reaches the earth's surface, it forms steam.

At the Geysers, wells were drilled to bring this steam to the surface. It roars out of the ground and travels through pipes to the power generating plant. In the plant it spins turbines that produce electricity for a city of more than 500,000 people.

At the Geysers in northern California, wells were drilled to bring super-heated water to the earth's surface. At the surface the hot water forms steam and travels through pipes to a power plant.

Today, geologists are searching for more places to drill geothermal fields. The most likely spots lie where pockets of magma remain near the earth's surface.

Sometimes geologists locate these pockets of magma by checking temperatures of the earth's crust at different depths. If the temperature grows much hotter than normal as the depth increases, a pocket of magma may be causing the added heat. Then, if this area has enough rainfall each year, it might be a good place for a geothermal field. Hot water from such underground fields lies untapped in many places around the world.

Scientists have learned much about magma pockets and how to use the energy they produce. In the years to come, their knowledge should increase rapidly as new geothermal fields are opened. Geothermal fields may even be drilled on or close to active volcanoes.

Future Energy Sources

Tapping nature's steam and hot water is just a beginning. If the tremendous heat of magma, itself, could be tapped, the energy produced would be far greater than that from steam and hot water.

Volcanologists already have attempted to use pockets of magma as energy sources. To succeed in this work, their equipment must operate in temperatures as high as 2,200°F (1,200°C). They are looking for different approaches to capture the energy from this red-hot source.

Some volcanologists believe that someday it may

be possible to capture the energy of erupting volcanoes. When Krakatoa erupted in 1883, it made a noise heard 3,000 miles (5,000 kilometers) away. Energy that transferred to the ocean from this eruption caused giant sea waves which killed thousands of people. If this energy could have been captured, thousands of people could have been helped rather than killed.

In the Ring of Fire, one volcano or another is nearly always erupting. The amount of energy released from even the smallest of these volcanic eruptions is enormous. In the oceans, underwater eruptions also release huge amounts of energy.

The world's volcanic hot spots form a challenging frontier. Scientists have much to learn before they can make use of the energy of magma. In time, though, they may find ways to capture the energy of volcanic eruptions on land and in the ocean. Perhaps you will be a member of a scientific team assigned to this exciting mission!

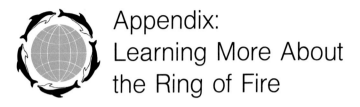

Appendix:
Learning More About
the Ring of Fire

The following activities will help you to learn more about the Ring of Fire. Choose one to begin working on today.

1. Read a book about the 1980 eruption of Mount St. Helens. (See Selected Bibliography.) Why did this volcano erupt so violently? What do you think we learned from this eruption that can help people in the future?

2. Visit a museum or rock shop. Ask the curator or dealer to help you locate rocks that came from a volcano. Find samples of as many kinds as you can, such as pumice and volcanic glass. If you live in or visit volcanic areas, you may find small volcanic rocks to start a collection.

3. Draw a map of the Pacific Ocean. Mark the places where well-known volcanoes (such as Krakatoa, in Indonesia) have erupted. Label and write something interesting about each volcano, such as its size. Mark the Hawaiian Islands and show the order in which each island moved across the hot spot in the mid-Pacific Ocean.

4. Start a scrapbook about volcanoes. Include clippings from newspapers about the eruptions or possible eruptions of volcanoes anywhere in the world. Include the date of each clipping.

 Glossary

active volcano—a volcano that has erupted in recent years

ash—melted volcanic rock that cooled and formed sand-sized pieces when it was thrown out into the air by an eruption

bombs—melted volcanic rock that cooled and formed large pieces of rock when it was thrown out into the air

caldera (kal-DEHR-uh)—a huge pit on top of a volcano formed by the collapse of its center, or cone

cinder cone—a cone-shaped volcano that forms when ash, cinders, and bombs pile up around the vent

cinders—melted volcanic rock that cooled and formed pebble-sized pieces when it was thrown out into the air

composite volcano—a volcano, such as Mount St. Helens, that has erupted in different ways at different times

core—used here to describe the innermost layer of the earth

crater—the bowl-shaped opening of a volcano where volcanic materials come out

crust—used here to describe the outer layer of the earth

dome—used here to describe a volcano in which the vent has been covered by a mushroom-shaped cap made of hardened lava

dormant volcano—a volcano that has erupted in modern times but has not been active in recent years

earthquake—a shaking or trembling of the earth that is volcanic or tectonic (resulting from changes in the earth's crust) in origin

erode—to wear away by the action of water, wind, or glacial ice

eruption (ih-RUHP-shun)—the sudden release of lava or other volcanic materials from the vent of a volcano

extinct (ik-STINKT) volcano—a volcano that has not erupted within historic times and probably will not erupt again

fire fountain—an unusually mild, fiery eruption

fissure (FISH-uhr)—a narrow opening or crack of considerable length and depth

fossil fuels—fuels, such as coal, oil, and natural gas, that come from living things

fracture (FRAK-chur) line—a long crack or break in the earth's surface

geologist (jee-AHL-uh-jist)—a scientist who studies the history of the earth and its life as recorded in its rocks

geothermal (jee-oh-THUR-muhl) power—energy produced by tapping the heat of the earth's interior, such as geothermal steam

geyser (GY-zer)—a spring that sends up jets of heated water and steam

glacier (GLAY-shur)—a large body of ice moving slowly down a slope or valley or spreading outward on a land surface

Gulf Stream—a warm ocean current flowing north from the Gulf of Mexico that merges with the North Atlantic Current near Newfoundland

harmonic tremor (har-MAHN-ik TREM-uhr)—a long, steady earthquake caused by the movement of magma under the earth's crust

hot spring—a spring having waters warmer than 98°F (37°C)

lagoon (luh-GOON)—a shallow pond, channel, or sound near or connected with a larger body of water

lava—molten rock that flows out of a volcanic vent during an eruption

magma (MAHG-muh)—melted rock below the earth's surface

mantle—the layer of the earth between the crust and core

Mediterranean (mehd-uh-tuh-RAY-nee-uhn) Belt—a belt of active volcanoes that stretches from southern Europe to central Asia

molten (MOHLT-ehn)—made into a liquid by heat

mud slide—used here to describe mixed water, volcanic materials, and soil moving rapidly down a volcano's slope

oceanographer (oh-shuh-NOG-reh-fer)—a person who uses scientific methods to explore and study the ocean

peninsula (puh-NIHN-suh-luh)—an area of land almost surrounded by water and connected to a larger body of land

pillow—used here to mean an extension of lava that has cooled and hardened on the outside but is still hot liquid inside

plates—used here to describe the pieces of the earth's crust and upper mantle; plates fit closely together and move slowly

plate tectonics (tek-TAHN-iks)—a scientific theory that explains why volcanoes, earthquakes, and mountains are found in certain areas of the world

plume—a hot spot in the earth's crust where magma sometimes breaks out

pumice (PUM-ihs)—a light, glassy volcanic rock filled with small holes

rift—a long, deep break, or fault, in the earth's crust

riftmeter—an instrument for measuring rifts

Ring of Fire—a belt along the edge of the Pacific Ocean where volcanoes and earthquakes often occur

sea-floor spreading—ridges formed on the ocean floor where magma pushes upward and forces the earth's plates apart

seamount—an underwater volcano

seismograph (SYZ-muh-graf)—an instrument that measures vibrations in the earth caused by earthquakes

shield volcano—a gently sloping volcanic mountain built up from eruptions of lava

silica (SIHL-uh-kuh)—a fine sand produced in large amounts by explosive eruptions

subduction (sub-DUHK-shun)—the process in which one of the earth's plates moves over the edge of another plate, causing it to bend downward into the mantle

Sundra Strait—a strait between Sumatra and Java, connecting the Java Sea and the Indian Ocean

tiltmeter—an instrument that measures the swelling in a volcanic mountain or other active area in the earth's crust

tsunami (soo-NAHM-ee)—giant, fast-moving ocean waves caused by a nearby volcanic eruption

turbine—a machine having a rotor, usually with vanes or blades, and driven by pressure of a moving fluid such as water

vent—used here to mean an opening in a volcano where steam and volcanic materials come out

volcano—a place where magma pushes out of a vent in the earth's crust; also, the cone, or mountain, formed by a volcanic eruption

volcanologist (vahl-kuh-NAHL-uh-jist)—a scientist who studies volcanoes

Selected Bibliography

Books

Fridriksson, Sturla. *Surtsey*. New York: Halsted Press, 1975.

Goldner, Kathryn, and Vogel, Carole. *Why Mount St. Helens Blew Its Top*. Minneapolis: Dillon Press, 1981.

Ritchie, David. *The Ring of Fire*. New York: Atheneum, 1981.

Scherman, Katharine. *Daughter of Fire: A Portrait of Iceland*. New York: Little, Brown, 1976.

Windley, Brian F. *The Evolving Continents*. New York: John Wiley, 1977.

Articles

Anderson, Tom. "A Revolution Called Plate Tectonics Has Given Us a Whole New Earth." *Smithsonian*, January 1975.

Bylinsky, Gene. "Water to Burn." *Fortune*, October 20, 1980.

Davenport, Marge. "Why a Sleeping Volcano Wakes." *Science Digest*, August 1980.

Earth Science. "Glaciers, Earthquakes, Volcanoes, and Fireballs." Summer 1982.

Hyman, Randall. "An Island Trembles Astride a Rift Where Our Planet's Crust is Forming." *Smithsonian*, January 1982.

Matthews, Samuel W. "The Changing Earth." *National Geographic*, January 1973.

National Geographic. Special Energy Issue. 1981.

Normark, William P.; Clague, David A.; and Moore, James G. "The Next Island." *Natural History*, December 1982.

Science News. "Predicting Volcanoes: A First?" October 11, 1975.

Scientific American. "The Dynamic Earth." September 1983 (entire issue).

Wellborn, Stanley N. "As Fallout from Angry Volcanoes Spreads." *U.S. News and World Report*, August 2, 1982.

Young, Gordon. "Hawaii, Land of Fire and Flowers." *National Geographic*, March 1975.

Index

About the Author

Alice Gilbreath is the author of eighteen previous books for young people during a twenty-year writing career. Her wide-ranging interests have led her to write about numerous subjects, from beginning crafts to the defensive techniques of animals.

"In writing this book," says the author, "I have tried to share with young people not only the awesome power of erupting volcanoes and the destruction they cause, but also the positive side of these eruptions. Materials brought to the earth's surface by volcanoes enrich the lives of people everywhere, and they help us to discover more about this marvelous planet we live on."

Ms. Gilbreath attended Trinity University in San Antonio, the University of Tulsa, and the College of Idaho. She lives in Bartlesville, Oklahoma.